KT-579-539

re-using & recycling

Metal

Ruth Thomson

Photography by Neil Thomson

W
FRANKLIN WATTS

B79 237 710 2

First published in 2006 by
Franklin Watts
338 Euston Road
London NW1 3BH

Franklin Watts Australia
Hachette Children's Books
Level 17/207 Kent Street
Sydney NSW 2000

Text copyright © Ruth Thomson 2006
Photographs © Neil Thomson 2006

Editor: Rachel Cooke
Design: Holly Mann
Art Director: Rachel Hamdi
Consultant: Diana Caldwell, Novelis

Additional photography
Thanks are due to the following for kind
permission to reproduce photographs:
Franklin Watts 6bl, 6c, 6br, 7, 9r; Atlas Copco
8br; B.H.P. Billiton 8tr, 8bl; Recycle now 14tl,
26br, 27bl; Novelis 15bl, 15tr, 15cr, 15br;
Ecoscene/Richard Glover 9l, Ecoscene/Miroslav
Imbrisevic 26t.

ISBN 0 7496 6100 3

A CIP catalogue record for this book is
available from the British Library.

Dewey Decimal Classification Number: 669

All rights reserved. No part of this publication
may be reproduced, stored in a retrieval system,
or transmitted in any form or by any other
means, electronic, mechanical, photocopy,
recording or otherwise, without the prior
written permission of the copyright owner.

Printed in China

Acknowledgements
The author and publisher wish to thank the
following people for their help with this book:
Luvuyo Nyathi and Peter Sudano; Vinod
Kumar Sharma, Michael Zhanje, Mark
Hoffman, Osama Ali, Cintia Cimbaluk,
Sue Adler and Mark Watson.

MILTON KEYNES LIBRARIES	
PET	J363.7288
1073557	14-Sep-07
£12.99	

Contents

What is metal like?   6

Mining for metals   8

Saving metal   10

Remade metal   12

Recycling cans   14

Canny transformations   16

Steely surprises   18

Bottle tops and ring pulls   20

Misprinted metal sheets   22

Container conversions   24

Recycling steel   26

Glossary   28

Guess what?   29

Useful websites   29

Index   30

Words printed in **bold** are explained in the glossary.

What is metal like?

Think how useful metal is. We travel in cars, trains and aeroplanes made of metal. Industries, hospitals and building sites use metal machines. Our homes are filled with metal sinks, cookers and radiators. There are over 70 sorts of metal.

Steel is hard and very strong. It is used for bridges, machines and beams for buildings.

Steel can be sharpened to make tools.

A steel knife has a sharp blade for cutting.

A steel drill bit has a sharp point.

Electricity travels well through **copper** cables.
Electricity comes into buildings along copper cables. Plastic flex, which does not **conduct** electricity, covers the wires.

Aluminium and steel can be rolled into thin, light sheets. The sheets are made into unbreakable food and drink cans.

IT'S A FACT

Mercury is the only metal which is liquid at room temperature. It **expands** quickly when it is heated and contracts as it cools, so it is used in **thermometers**.

Heat travels very quickly through metals.
Metal pots and pans heat up over a flame. They are useful for cooking food.

Gold, silver and **platinum** are rare precious metals. Jewellers use precious metals to make rings, necklaces, bracelets, earrings and brooches.

Turned to rust

Most **iron** and steel things rust if they are left out in the wet. They turn brown and flaky and begin to crumble into pieces.

Mining for metals

Most metals are found inside rocks. **Geologists** search for areas where rocks contain a lot of metal. These rocks are known as **ores**.

Metal bearing rock

Open pit mining

If the ore is near the surface, huge **excavators** remove the top layers of soil and rock and then scoop up the ore. Sometimes explosives blast hard ore into pieces.

Underground mining

Some ores lie deep underground. Miners dig a deep shaft with tunnels leading from it. They drill or blast the rocks to mine the ore.

As the wheel of the excavator turns, the scoops pick up ore.

IT'S A FACT

Only gold, silver, platinum and copper can be found in solid lumps of pure metal. These are known as nuggets.

Making iron

Iron is the most plentiful metal produced. Iron ore is crushed and heated with **coke** and **limestone** in a **blast furnace** to separate out the metal. Iron cracks easily, so it is used to make steel, which is far stronger.

Making steel

Molten iron is poured over scrap steel in a huge tilting container. A jet of pure oxygen blasts onto the liquid metal. This burns away most of the impurities to make steel.

LOOK AND SEE

Collect some everyday things made of metal. Discover whether they are iron or steel by putting a **magnet** over them. Only iron and steel objects are magnetic.

9

Saving metal

Most metal objects are hard-wearing and long-lasting. Things that one person no longer wants are usually in good enough condition for someone else to re-use.

For sale

All these second-hand metal items were on sale in a market. Can you recognise them all?

Old oil drums

People find all sorts of uses for empty oil drums.

Animal feed trough

Road Closed
No access to NY3.
Use NY50.

USE ME

Temporary road sign   Litter bin

Any old iron?

In many parts of the world, collectors wander city streets, buying any bits of old metal they find. They take the metal to a scrapyard.

A metal scrapyard

Scrap metal merchants sort the metal before they resell it. Builders buy pipes, rods, girders and gates. Craftworkers buy pieces of scrap metal to melt and shape into furniture, mirror frames and other objects.

Remade metal

In many countries, small metal workshops turn old **factory**-made objects into new, cheap household equipment.

Pots, pans and stoves

In Morocco, metal workers cut old steel water heaters and oil drums in half.

They fix on legs to make charcoal stoves.

They cut and shape pieces to make buckets.

They add handles to turn them into huge cooking pots.

An original oven

A washing machine drum has been turned into this portable oven. The food seller bakes sweet potatoes in it.

A glass holder

Factories often bind **bales** of goods with long metal strips. Once the bales are opened, the strips are thrown away. In Egypt, craftspeople re-use them to make holders for carrying glasses of hot tea.

Bicycle chain bits

Factories press bicycle chain out of metal sheets. The leftover sheets are full of holes. These are of no use to the factories, but metal craftspeople in India bend and shape them into useful things.

A bird cage

A shoe rack

Recycling cans

Steel food and aluminium drink cans can
be recycled to make new steel or aluminium.

Can banks

You can put
both steel and
aluminium cans
into can banks.
Magnets
separate out
the steel cans
at a recycling
centre.

Fine foil

Aluminium can be made into
thin sheets of foil, used for
food tubs, pie cases or
chocolate wrappers. You can
recycle foil,
but keep it
separate
from
cans.

YOU CAN HELP

Aluminium factories buy
empty cans, because they
can be used again and
again for making
more aluminium.

Raise money for your school,
a club or a charity by
collecting empty cans for
recycling (see addresses
on page 29).

• Check that the cans are made
of aluminium. They have a shiny
base, whereas the base of a steel
can looks dull.

• Aluminium cans are not magnetic.
Test the side of a can with a magnet.

REMEMBER!

Crush cans to save space in can banks.

Recycling aluminium cans

1. At a recycling centre, a heavy press squashes the empty drink cans together into bales.

3. The molten aluminium is poured into a **mould** and then cooled with water. The aluminium sets into a big block called an **ingot**.

4. Rollers flatten the ingot into a long sheet of very thin metal.

2. The bales go to a **foundry**, where they are shredded, cleaned and melted in a hot furnace along with raw materials.

5. New cans are punched from the sheet. These are filled with drink and sent to shops.

Canny transformations

In countries where new metal is expensive, empty steel drink cans are a cheap raw material for craftworkers. They are thin and easy to cut with hand tools.

Can collection

This South African craftsman designs dozens of things from drink cans, including belts, bowls, boxes and toys. Street children bring him more than half a million cans a year off the street. He pays for them by the sackful.

Christmas tree

It takes four cans to make an aeroplane.

Jewellery box

A shady visor

1. The craftsman washes the cans, cuts off the ends and slices the cans down one side.

2. He flattens the can pieces and cuts shapes out of them using a **template**.

3. He glues on a soft fabric lining.

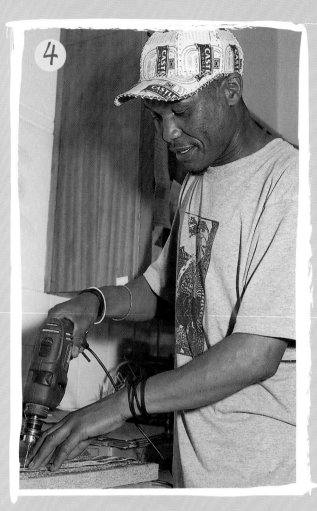

4. He drills holes at regular intervals along each piece of the visor.

5. He sews the pieces together with scrap telephone wire.

17

Steely surprises

In parts of Africa and India people create useful objects using the strong metal from empty glue or cooking oil cans.

Moneybox

Festive gifts

At the festival of Eid parents give their children money. In the weeks before Eid, some craftsmen in Egypt turn from making stoves and buckets to making money-boxes. Parents buy these to encourage their children to save.

Parents also buy their children toys made from cut-up cans.

Rattle

Tambourines

Kitchen equipment

Many people cannot afford new, factory-made kitchen tools. Instead, they buy cheaper ones, hand-crafted from food cans.

Grater

Funnel

Food scoop

Sieve

Kitchen tongs

Slotted spoon

Craftworkers also make tourist souvenirs.

Toy vehicles

Madagascans make toy vehicles from cans. Each family makes a different type, so they do not compete for sales.

Motorbike

Car

Crafty creatures

Zimbabweans make model animals.

Aeroplane

Chameleon

Crab

Duck

Bottle tops and ring pulls

Even the metal bottle tops and ring pulls from cans are re-used to make something new.

Making music

Threaded onto a piece of metal wire, the bottle tops clink and clank when you wave this shaker to and fro.

Shaker

Curious candlesticks

A bottle top is set into each of these Indian papier mâché candleholders for a candle to stand in.

More than a dozen bottle tops make up the column of this candlestick.

A surprising suitcase

Can you work out how many bottle tops make up this suitcase? The bottle tops are joined together with twisted wire.

One of a kind

A Brazilian bag maker threads strips of old fabric or leather through ring pulls to make one-off bags like these. The one on the left shows the Brazilian flag.

Jangling jewellery

A Jamaican jeweller squashed bottle tops flat to make these colourful earrings.

Ring pulls were threaded in pairs on a strip of rubber to make this unusual bracelet.

YOUR TURN

In many parts of the world, children play draughts in the sand or on a board, using bottle tops as counters.

Make your own draughts board.
- Draw a grid of 64 squares on some heavy card.
- Colour in alternate squares.
- Collect 24 bottle tops – it does not matter if they are not all the same.

Lay the bottle caps out to play. One player lays them top side up; the other lays them upside down.

Misprinted metal sheets

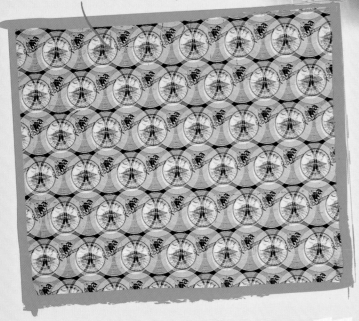

A sheet of
misprinted bottle tops

Steel cans and bottle
tops are made from large
sheets of steel. Before
a sheet is cut, the name
of a product is printed
all over it. If the name
is misprinted, the sheet
is rejected.

Metal craftsmen buy misprinted sheets very cheaply. They cut these up to make them into lamps, storage tins and other household things.

Dustpan from the Gambia

Lantern and candlestick from Morocco

Food scoop from India

Storage tin from Indonesia

Watering can from Morocco

Container conversions

People send goods across the sea in shipping containers. After some years, the huge containers are so battered by wind and waves, they are no longer usable for sea voyages. However, in South Africa, many are converted into buildings.

Changing containers

Workmen cut new windows and doors in the containers, fit new flooring and install electricity and water. Lorries transport the containers to an empty site. A crane lifts them in place.

A takeaway stall

This takeaway stall is a container fitted with a spit for roasting chickens, a fridge, a sink, a store cupboard and a serving hatch.

Township telephones

There are container phone shops on many street corners in the townships near Cape Town. Inside each one are five phone booths.

A spacious library

Three containers were joined together to make a spacious children's library.

Stacked studios

An English architect has designed apartments and studios made from containers stacked several storeys high. Notice how the original doors have become the sides of the balconies.

Recycling steel

Most steel is recycled into new steel. This saves the energy used to mine and heat iron ore, as well as saving very useful metal. It also helps the **environment** because the metal is not buried at a **landfill site**.

Reduced to scrap

Millions of cars are recycled every year – far more than anything else made of metal.

Scrapyards break up the cars, stripping out any parts that can be used again.

Magnets separate the steel from other metals. The steel is then recycled.

Cars piled up in a scrapyard

Around and around

Absolutely everything made of steel contains some recycled steel. A new car may contain steel that was once part of a washing machine or a can.

When cans are recycled, the steel might be used in new cans, in a steel girder for a building or for a fridge.

YOU CAN HELP

Recycle all your steel food and pet food cans and aerosols.

- Rinse cans before recycling. Beware of any sharp edges.

- Put the lids inside the cans.

- Squash cans as flat as you can.

REMEMBER!

- Do NOT squash aerosols.

- Remove the plastic top.

- Put the aerosols in the can bank just as they are.

aerosol

Glossary

aluminium a hard, light, silvery-white metal, often used to make drink cans and foil

bale a large bundle

blast furnace a tall tower lined with fireproof bricks where iron is melted at a very high heat

coke a fuel made by heating coal in an oven

conduct to transfer heat or electricity easily from place to place

copper a soft, brownish-red metal that does not rust

environment the world around us – the land, sea and air

excavator a machine used for digging something out of the ground

expand to grow bigger

factory a building where things are made in large numbers using machines

foundry a building where metal is melted and made into new things

geologist someone who studies the Earth's rocks, minerals and soil to find out what they are made of

gold a pale yellow, soft, shiny metal

ingot a hard block of metal cast in a mould

iron a very common grey metal

landfill site a huge pit in the ground where crushed rubbish is buried

limestone a chalky white rock

magnet an object that attracts iron or steel

melt to turn from a solid to a liquid

mercury a heavy, silvery, liquid metal

molten melted into a liquid by great heat

mould a hollow shaped container into which liquid metal is poured, so that the metal takes on that shape when it cools and hardens

ore a rock that metals are found in

platinum a silvery-white precious metal

scrap metal scraps of iron or other metal, only of use for remelting

silver a shiny, grey precious metal

steel a strong, hard-wearing metal made mostly from iron

template an outline shape that you can draw around to make the same shape over and over again

thermometer an instrument for measuring how hot or cold something is

Guess what?

- Around 6 per cent of the weight of your household rubbish is metal cans.

- People in the UK use 5 billion aluminium cans per year.

- Remelting aluminium uses only 5 per cent of the energy needed to make new aluminium.

- Steel cans are often called tin cans, because they have a very thin layer of tin (another type of metal) on the inside. This prevents the cans from going rusty and ruining the food inside.

Useful websites

www.alupro.org.uk (Aluminium Packaging Recycling Organisation) Information about aluminium and can recycling, as well as the 'cash for cans' scheme.

www.ollierecycles.com
A fun, interactive site for children, which includes information and tips on recycling steel and aluminium cans.

www.recycle-more.co.uk
Games, information and advice about recycling at home and at school, including how to find your local recycling centre.

www.recyclezone.org.uk
Activities, games and information on recycling in general.

www.scrib.org (The Steel Can Recycling Information Bureau) Offers free resources about steel recycling – including booklets, posters and fridge magnets.

www.thinkcans.com
Information about the value of aluminium, the lifecycle of a drink can and how to raise money by recycling cans. Activities and games for teachers and pupils.

Index

aeroplane 6, 16, 19
aerosol 27
aluminium 7, 14, 15, 29

bag 21
bale 13, 15
bicycle chain 13
blast furnace 9
bottle top 20, 21, 22
bridge 6
building 6, 24, 25, 27

can
    aerosol 27
    drink 7, 14, 15, 16, 17, 20
    food 7, 14, 19, 27
    steel 7, 14, 16, 22, 27, 29
can bank 14, 27
car 6, 26, 27
containers 24, 25
copper 6, 9

electricity 6, 24
environment 26

excavator 8

foil 14
foundry 15
furnace 15

geologist 8
gold 7, 9

ingot 15
iron 7, 9, 11, 26
iron ore 9, 26

jeweller 7, 21

landfill site 26

magnet 9, 14, 26
mercury 7
metal sheet 13, 22, 23
mining 8
moneybox 18
mould 15

nugget 9

oil drum 10, 12
ore 8, 9, 26
oxygen 9

platinum 7, 9

recycling 14, 15, 26, 27
ring pull 20, 21
rock 8
rust 7, 29

scrapyard 11, 26
silver 7, 9
steel 6, 7, 9, 12, 22, 26, 27

template 17
thermometer 7
tin 29
tool 6, 16
    kitchen 19
toy 16, 18, 19

wire 6, 17, 20
workshop 12